Gangs and Drugs

TOOKIE SPEAKS OUT AGAINST GANG VIOLENCE™

Stanley "Tookie" Williams

with Barbara Cottman Becnel

The Rosen Publishing Group's

New York

Published in 1996 by The Rosen Publishing Group, Inc.
29 East 21st Street, New York, NY 10010

First Edition

Book design: Kim Sonsky

Photo credits: Cover © Maratea/International Stock; front cover inset, back cover, and p. 4 © J. Patrick Forden; pp. 7, 11, 12 by Maria Moreno; pp. 8, 15 by Sarah Friedman; p. 16 © Bill Stanton/International Stock; p. 19 by Kim Sonsky; p. 20 by Seth Dinnerman.

Williams, Stanley.
   Gangs and drugs / Stanley "Tookie" Williams, with Barbara Cottman Becnel.
   p. cm. — (Tookie speaks out against gang violence)
   Includes index.
   Summary: One of the founders of the Crips, a Los Angeles gang, tells the reader about the dangers of gang life, particularly of getting involved with drug use and drug dealing.
   ISBN 0-8239-2348-7
   1. Gangs—United States—Juvenile literature. 2. Drug abuse—United States—Juvenile literature. 3. Crips (Gang)—Juvenile literature. [1. Gangs. 2. Drug abuse. 3. Crips (Gang).] I. Becnel, Barbara Cottman. II. Title. III. Series: Williams, Stanley. Tookie speaks out against gang violence.
HV6439.U5W54 1996
364.1'06'60973—dc20
                                          96-6991
                                               CIP
                                             AC

Manufactured in the United States of America

Contents

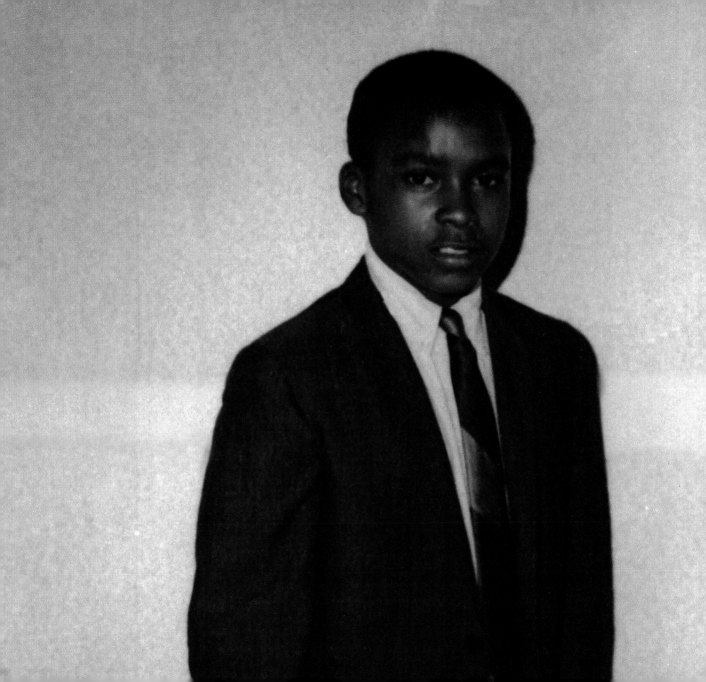

The Hustlers of South Central

When I was young, I liked hanging out with the older guys in my South Central Los Angeles **'hood** (HOOD). Many of them were **hustlers** (HUSS-lerz) who made money by doing bad things like stealing and selling drugs.

I was named after my father, Stanley "Tookie" Williams. He didn't teach me what was right or wrong because he wasn't around. And my mom worked all the time. So I learned from the hustlers in my 'hood. But I learned more about doing wrong than doing right. By the time I was 13, I was using drugs.

◀ *When Tookie moved to South Central, he trusted his new friends. He didn't know they would teach him to do bad things.*

Sniffing Glue

The first drug I ever used was glue. I started sniffing glue because my friends did. I wanted them to think I was **down** (DOWN), really cool.

Glue was easy to steal. We didn't have much money, so it was a free way for us to get **high** (HI). Sniffing glue made me feel weird. I lost track of time. I also got into a lot of trouble. When my friends and I got high, we threw rocks at car windows, stole from stores, and fought other kids.

Sometimes kids try drugs because they think it makes them look cool. ▶

Meeting Raymond

At 17, I was still sniffing glue, stealing, and fighting. But now I fought older kids who belonged to gangs. That was how I met Raymond Washington, a teen from the east side of South Central. Raymond wanted me, him, and our **homeboys** (HOME-boyz) to start a gang. We wanted to protect ourselves from being hurt by other gangs. We called our new gang the Crips.

Back then, the Crips didn't sell drugs. But many of us used drugs. We thought we were down, but we were hurting ourselves.

◀ *Smart kids avoid drugs. They know that using drugs will hurt them.*

Getting Sick

I sniffed so much glue that pink spots popped up on my lips and my face. I was scared that my face would stay that color. My mother took me to the doctor. I was treated with **radiation** (ray-dee-AY-shun). A big machine beamed x-rays into my body.

The doctor's treatment worked. My skin turned back to its natural brown color. I learned a lesson about how drugs can hurt you. I made glue sniffing off-limits for my homeboys, the Crips.

Sniffing glue can hurt you in many ways. It can make you feel sick to your stomach. ▶

Becoming Addicted

The lesson I learned about how bad it is to use drugs didn't last long. I started smoking **marijuana** (mayr-i-WAN-na) or "weed" and using a drug called PCP or "sherm." I was **addicted** (a-DIK-ted) to sherm. Being addicted to a drug means that you need to use that drug more than you need anything else, even food.

I acted crazy when I was addicted to sherm. It was a bad time for me.

◀ *Many people don't realize how easy it is to become addicted to drugs.*

13

Coping with Fear

Gang members use drugs for many reasons. I used drugs because I wanted to belong. A lot of gang members use drugs because they're scared of doing all the bad things that they have to do. They use drugs to make them feel brave and tough and strong enough to hurt someone or commit a crime.

But relying on drugs doesn't make you brave. It makes you foolish because you're not listening to yourself. You know that what you're doing is wrong. But you use drugs so you can do it anyway.

Some people use drugs to try to feel strong and brave. ▶

Set-Tripping

Drugs became important to gangs for another reason. Selling drugs was a way to earn a lot of money. But selling drugs is against the law. So is using them.

Every gang wanted to make money. The Crips split into smaller groups. Each group was called a gang set. Soon Crips fought with other Crips over drugs, money, and power. We called that **set-tripping** (SET-tripping). Many of my homeboys were arrested or killed because of drug-dealing and set-tripping.

◄ *Many gang members are hurt or killed because of set-tripping.*

Life as a Drug Slinger

Whether you're a gang member or not, **slinging** (SLING-ing)—selling—drugs is a life of danger and violence. You worry about the police putting you in jail. You worry about others stealing your drugs and money. And you worry about someone killing you for what you have.

People can make a lot of money slinging drugs. But it's not worth it. They won't stay free from prison, or stay alive, long enough to enjoy it.

Some people forget that their lives are more important than making money. ▶

Smart Kids Avoid Drugs

You have to be smart to stay away from drugs and gangs. Being smart means that you trust yourself and listen to yourself. There will be kids who will try to talk you into doing things that hurt you, like using or selling drugs, or joining a gang. Being smart means that what you think is right and wrong means more to you than what your homeboys think. It also means that if you don't know what to do when someone pushes you to do something wrong, you know to go to someone you trust for help.

◀ *Being smart means asking for help if someone tries to get you to use drugs.*

Wanting the Best

Drugs and gangs won't make you happy. Happiness comes from feeling good about yourself. You must believe in yourself and trust that you know right from wrong. You have to be strong enough to be by yourself, if you have to, and to stay away from kids who could get you into trouble.

I want the best for you. I want you to feel as good as I feel since I gave up drugs and gang life. But first you must want the very best for yourself. So be smart. Don't let anyone talk you into doing drugs.

Glossary

addicted (a-DIK-ted) Needing a drug.

to be **down** (DOWN) To be ready to do anything because your homeboys expect you to.

high (HI) Feeling different than normal.

homeboy (HOME-boy) Friend or partner.

'hood (HOOD) Slang word for neighborhood.

hustler (HUSS-ler) Person who makes money from doing bad things like stealing, selling, and using drugs.

marijuana (mayr-i-WAN-na) Drug that is often smoked; also called "weed."

radiation (ray-dee-AY-shun) X-rays that are beamed into a person's body to get rid of a rash or disease.

set-tripping (SET-trip-ping) When gang sets fight each other.

slinging (SLING-ing) Slang word for selling drugs.

Index